OR ELSE

poems by

Diana Loercher Pazicky

Finishing Line Press
Georgetown, Kentucky

OR ELSE

ACKNOWLEDGMENTS

Beauty in Word and Image, James A. Michener Museum exhibition catalogue
(2013)
Schuylkill Valley Journal: "Venus Redux" (2013), "Else" (2014), "Animal
Lover" (2015), "The Weeping Beech" (2015), "The Arms of Morpheus"
(2015).
Moonstone Press: "The Weeping Beech," (2017)
U.S. 1 Work Sheets: "Extremities," (2018)
Exit 13: "Shooting the Leopard" (2018)

Publisher: Leah Maines
Editor: Christen Kincaid
Cover Art: Diana Loercher Pazicky
Author Photo: Ed Pazicky
Cover Design: Leah Huete

Printed in the USA on acid-free paper.
Order online: www.finishinglinepress.com
        also available on amazon.com

Author inquiries and mail orders:
Finishing Line Press
P. O. Box 1626
Georgetown, Kentucky 40324
U. S. A.

Table of Contents

For Ed, my rock

*Special thanks to Dr. Christopher Bursk
for his workshop and inspiration.*

I.

Else

Derived from the Old English elles, *meaning other*

I am tantalized by Else.
No, not Elsie, Elsa, or Elise,
but Else, a word warranting capitalization,
proper nounhood in its own right.

Else encompasses the unknown,
the alternatives that impinge
upon our constricted lives.
Else, else, else…

Leaves rustling outside the window
whispering the susurrus of desire—
Or else! Redolent with danger,
the wail of sirens in the night time.

Else is an enchanted island
beyond clipped horizons
inhabited by sirens singing,
Where else? Who else? What else?

Today I dare not answer
except in waking dreams,
else I lose my way and drown.
Tomorrow is something else.

Extremities

There is in capes a wildness born of shape—
attenuated promontories thrusting
like swords into the sea, peninsulas
with beckoning fingers, alluring names:
Cape Horn, Cape Byron, Cape Fear, Cape
Wrath, Cape Farewell, Cape of Good Hope.

I once walked the length of the Cape of St. Vincent
in Sagres, Portugal, the southernmost tip of Europe
where Prince Henry the Navigator set sail
to the New World. The wind was so fierce it
pummeled me, whipped my hair, tore my clothes,
as I stumbled down the rocky terrain, feared
being blown off the towering cliff,
plunging into the turgid Atlantic
beating at the rock below,
eating away the foundation.

I pushed on to the tip, beheld an ocean
so vast it seemed to stretch to infinity,
grasped why the Romans called it the Holy Promontory,
why it was once considered the end of the known world,
imagined how Henry must have felt when he stood
at this most extreme point where land and sea meet
and extend an irresistible invitation to discovery.

Animal Lover

In her mind's eye, clouded with grief,
she watches her cat pad up the driveway to greet her,
his body swaying side to side,
the bronze luster of his fur shining in the sunlight.

How paltry the loss of her cat compared
to the death march of entire species—
the Arctic polar bear, the Siberian tiger,
the Madagascar tortoise, the African elephant.

Yet, as she conjures up his image
curled on a cushion in the summer sun,
she mourns him more deeply,
his rumbling purr and woody scent,
her hand stroking his glossy fur,
the heft of his muscular body.

She mourns him as she cannot mourn
other animals, people she does not know,
even people she does know.
Her husband asks her in jest
if she would mourn as deeply for him.
She smiles, hesitates a second too long.

Meditation on the Pencil, While Grading Papers

I have given up on ink,
pens that smear and reek,
the violence of the colors.
Crossed out, whited out,
the delible still indelible
leaves permanent stains,
like bruises or dried blood.

The pencil allows one to reconsider,
stop time and go back,
undo that hasty judgment,
edit out the lies,
assay the truth.

Erasers are soft, forgiving,
leave only a faint smudge,
a chance to correct oneself
before presuming
to judge another.

The pencil erases,
begins again
its clean
straight
line.

The Weeping Beech

Opposite the campus chapel
looms a weeping beech
shaped like a giant mushroom,
inchoate mass of bent branches,
pendulous leaves dripping
a torrential rain of tears.
I enter through thick foliage
clawing at me like an animal.
Cool and moist under the canopy,
I am a pagan come to worship.

The trunk is elephantine in girth,
branches extended, mottled in color,
like bloated, elastic pythons
and grotesque as gargoyles.
Students have carved their initials,
hung wishes on scraps of white paper
attached to branches by strands of string:
I wish you would fall back in love with me.
I wish my Dad was still here and I was still whole.
I wish I was able to breathe.

I sit in the crook of the trunk,
track the lines of roots that lace the ground,
lead down to the earth's dark secrets.
Above, twining branches form their own script,
calligraphed words written in an arcane language
I cannot read but almost understand.

The Porch

Those hot nights in summer before air conditioning
when the air was heavy and spongy as wet foam,
my parents let me sleep on the screened-in porch.

The porch was small, like me, just big enough
for a couple of chairs and a twin bed
covered with a gaudy Indian spread.

I imagined I was stranded on a desert island
learning from the animals how to survive.
At night it was silent except for the cicadas,

a refuge from the complicated sounds inside
and from the heat, relieved by uncanny breezes
coming from nowhere and blowing breaths

of cool air, wafting the thick scent
of wisteria over my body, like unguent.
At dawn I awakened to sunlight seeping,

the urgent buzz of bumble bees feasting,
the reveille of the birds, an unwelcome
reminder: time to go back inside.

Going Bananas

When I buy bananas I think of my mother,
remember the story she told me as a child
about the time she was at the market,
picked up a bunch of ripe bananas,
was about to put them in the cart
when out crawled to greet her
a large, leggy, furry tarantula.

She screamed, dropped the bananas,
and was surrounded by onlookers
shocked at the unwelcome apparition
of a stowaway hidden in the crates.
They marveled that a bunch of bananas,
banal and benign, could harbor such horror
while a clerk stabbed the spider with a knife.

My mother admonished me
never to pick up bananas
without inspecting them,
as if they were explosives.
I was already convinced, am still,
that beneath any innocent façade,
mortal danger may dwell.

Shooting the Leopard

Night sends out its call to the cats.

The leopard crosses the savannah,
his stride and golden eyes unwavering,
intent on a destination known only to him.

His spotted coat reflects the waning light.
Taut muscles ripple in rhythm,
sway with his luminous body.

He has not yet noticed
three hulking, steel beasts
blocking his path.

The guides train spotlights on him.
He pauses, takes in the scene, sits down,
far more dignified than the species opposite.

Eyes lock on him, cameras click wildly.
We have become the predator,
and this is the perfect shot.

His eyes close; he falls asleep.
Our eyes close too
blinded by the flash.

SS Enchantment of the Seas

A propeller fails and the ship,
a wounded sea serpent,
drags in its wake
a crooked tail of foam.

At night the ship strains southward
against slapping, pummeling waves.
We toss in our narrow beds,
hear the creaks, feel the shudders,
as the ship struggles against the wind,
a bird with only one wing.

What is this nautical monster,
this bloated white behemoth,
this mechanized Moby Dick
that never dives or breathes
but sucks its life from engines
and belches gaseous fumes?

Then the catastrophic images—
the second propeller failing,
casting us adrift,
the ship breaking apart—
too few life boats—
and finally the crucible:
who lives, who dies?

In the morning when the sun shines,
we lie on deck and exchange
the nightmare for daydreams
of riding whales and porpoises,
forget we sit on a razor of metal
barely slicing the surface of the sea.

Watching Dressage

The rider: black jacket, hat, boots,
white breeches and gloves matching
the white Lipizzaner he sits astride.
He: with the help of two bits, four reins,
spurs, and a whip if needed, puts her
through unnatural, Olympian paces.

She: trots in place, sometimes with a pause,
haunches quivering, before putting down hooves,
canters with lengthened, then shortened stride,
makes flying changes of lead at canter,
half passes on the diagonal, ricochets
forward, sideways at the same time,
almost tips over her hooves—
the climax, "airs above the ground,"
a series of athletic jumps in midair
in time to Strauss waltzes.

The goal is to look effortless,
for rider and horse to move
in perfect synchronicity,
strain on the horse imperceptible
while the rider sends subtle signals.
They say the horses are born to it,
that they like the discipline,
the challenge, the performance.

My eyes glaze and I am the horse—
kick, buck, bolt—throw the rider—
jump the fence—gallop—
bridle, reins, stirrups flying,
not caring where I'm going,
not caring if they catch me,
caught only in the moment,
in the rapture of running,
without a rider, without rules.

Captives

When I approach, two Oscar fish surge,
fins fanning wildly like sails in the wind.
They stare at me, perhaps hoping I'll feed them,
perhaps to break up the Sisyphean monotony
of a journey back and forth between glass walls,
tantalizing barricades to vistas they cannot reach.
Conjuring up hamsters spinning on the wheel,
or the definition of insanity, they hypnotize.

"He" (I assume from his large size)
is a blend of lacquered black and brown
streaked with magisterial gold lamé.
His bulging eyes are dark except when light
catches them, uses its alchemy to turn them
into golden beams flashing on and off
as he executes slow, graceful pirouettes
propelled by pale gray fins, translucent veils.

"She" is a delicate, miniature version of him,
ebony but decorated with iridescent speckles
of emerald, gold, and turquoise, looking like
a peacock that dove by mistake into the water.
Lithe and limber, she moves faster than he,
flutters the gossamer filigree of her fins and tail
with nervous energy, as she circles the tank
and the lump of fake black driftwood.

I wonder, do they pass by
in oblivion, or do they depend
on each other, at the very least
for the mere solace of presence?
Would one miss the other if it died?
Or is this just another bad marriage
in which lonely couples circle,
swim their separate channels?

II.

Venus Redux

Venus had nothing on you, Mom.
Beyond the eyes of the child
I once was, and still am,
I see in your perfect naked body
the proportions of Praxiteles,
the divinity of Botticelli,
the voluptuousness of Titian,
the eroticism of Bronzino,
the narcissism of Velasquez.

Beneath these representations I see
only the memory of your body—
your perfect white skin
your perfect white breasts
your perfect white belly—
all of them begging to be touched
as you paraded naked through the house,
and I hung back in the shadows, furious,
knowing such perfection could never be mine.

Arachne Talks Back

Athena, why begrudge
a poor peasant girl
such a paltry victory?

Because I dared to challenge you, goddess?
Because I wove a tapestry so tight, intricate,
with threads that glittered like gemstones,
you could not bear to be outshone?

Crueler than your blows from the shuttle,
the needles piercing the thin fabric
of my fresh, radiant, youthful skin,
was your slashing of my masterpiece.

I hung myself by a rope thicker
than the fine silk thread
that tethered me to my talent,
and turned into a spider:

> *I spin, I spin, I spin*
> *perfect webs, trap flies*
> *on which I feed, devour,*
> *imagine each one is you.*
> *Fuel myself, lay eggs*
> *in a sac where they hatch,*
> *breed long after you*
> *are but a vague memory.*

The Red Shoes

As a child, I saw the movie,
watched Moira Shearer, bewitched
by a pair of shiny red shoes,
spin through the streets like a harlot,
flaunt her profane slippers in church.
Cursed to dance to exhaustion or death,
she struggled to remove them,
but they clung, tight as her skin.
She begged to have her feet cut off,
and away they pranced into the forest.

I did not understand,
but knew, as we know things
we do not wish to know,
and grew up fearing red shoes,
did not buy a pair till my twenties:
shiny high heels with flirty bows.

But I never wore them dancing.

The Arms of Morpheus

You descended to me nightly
a blazing comet in human form,
drove off the furies with your fiery wand,
demons biting at my brain like flies.

Then you came to me softly,
fell hard upon me, broke me,
left me in oblivion to dream.
But now, faithless lover,

I lie sleepless,
rigid on this bed,
once soft feathers
now a slab of stone,

stare into the darkness
longing for your fire,
your incandescent hands
upon my shivering, pale body,

upon my eyelids your merciful touch
foreshadowing final sweet sleep.

Poseidon's Wet Dream

Even Poseidon needs a vacation now and then.
Tired of galloping his steeds over the ocean,
churning up waves, from swells to tsunamis,
tired of changing tides, shifting currents,
he hangs up his signature trident,
rides his chariot to the Caribbean,
calms the waters to a gentle chop,
leans back and dozes in the sun.

One day off the coast of St. Lucia,
marveling at the lush green
nourished by centuries of volcanic ash,
and at the towering Pitons,
twin peaks soaring into the sky,
elongated mountains stolen
from the brush of Modigliani,

Poseidon falls asleep, dreams
the slender Pitons' soft fir trees,
are fertile young women
with perky, pointed breasts
spraying milk into the sky
in the form of white clouds.

Waking up in a spasm of delight,
Poseidon, inspired by the muse
and the island's iridescent colors,
finger-paints twin rainbows
arcing over the island
and sliding into the sea.

Amazed, tourists on the cruise ship
stare, take photographs, wonder
mirage, miracle, physics?
Never imagine Poseidon.

Nude Beach

On a French beach in the Caribbean
we're sprawled on lounge chairs,
my husband in his Hawaiian surfer trunks,
I in my one-piece "Miracle" suit.

Next to us perch an even older couple.
She is topless, bikinied below,
with the body of a young girl
in the carapace of an old woman.
He is muscular and sports a thong
too minuscule to matter.
They get up to play paddle ball.

On parade the full array
of bellies and bulges,
corporeal anomalies—
a textured tapestry
of smooth and wrinkled skin,
the gravitational droop
and lift of breasts,
one man totally nude.

As natural as water sprites
cavorting in the sand,
they embarrass us,
inspire us (almost!) to strip,
run naked down the beach,
breasts, buttocks, genitals bobbing
in rhythm with the breaking waves.

A God for All Seasons

Maybe the Greeks had it right after all
with their pantheon of deities
animating nature with their caprices.
Take Zeus, the supreme Lord
of the Sky, Rain God, Cloud Gatherer
hurling thunderbolts like a naughty little boy.

Zeus, progenitor of today's weatherman,
not the meteorologist but the disasterologist,
displacing the God of Creation
and wreaking havoc all over the earth—
droughts, floods, hurricanes, cyclones,
tsunamis, fires, blizzards, earthquakes,
and most recently global warming—
without giving a fig for the consequences.

Imagine the horny old lecher
cavorting around Mount Olympus,
pursuing women to take to bed
and taunting his furious wife.
Zeus, as profligate in his desires
as his passion for destruction.

The Furies

The past hangs heavy,
its high humidity
so thick you can touch it,
choke on it like cotton.

Then the night demons come,
dreaded, not unexpected,
drones announcing their arrival
with a creeping, piercing buzz.

Wily descendants of the furies
who punished sinners directly,
they change their tactics,
infiltrate the human mind,
a far greater source of misery
than any pain they could inflict.

Flying under the radar,
Regret, Remorse, Guilt
surprise attack, awaken,
leave us shaken, sleepless.
How well they have taught us
to punish ourselves.

III.

The Woods

Spring, Delaware Canal, Pennsylvania

I dare not go down to the woods
where trees wave to me like fans,
branches beckon like fingers,
pull me against my will.

The woods
               spread along the canal
where I canoed for days at sunset
with my son to study a beaver lodge,
both of us eager, exultant.

The woods
               where he and his friend
played tag, hide and seek, threw the ball
for our Lab, splashed in the mud
and the water.

The woods
               where I led the boys,
the dog racing ahead, behind,
along the rough-hewn path
through its bushes and brambles,

to reach the stream gurgling over rocks
that drenched our feet as we slipped,
then onward to the so-called "cliffs,"
the rocky mound curved like a half moon

hanging over a clearing where we clambered
over rocks the Lenape once climbed,
imagined ceremonies, listened for drumbeats,
searched for arrow heads, anything left behind.

Then our sanctuary,
                              a bamboo forest
packed so tight we could barely squeeze
between the trees. We did not speak,
listened to the sacred hush

broken only by dry leaves' crackle
and slender stalks rubbing together
in response to the whispering breeze
cooling our tired, sweaty bodies.

I dare not go down to the woods,
miss too much those not there,
all that remains without them,
all that might be gone.

Seaside Victorian

The house she inhabited
slowly inhabited her.
Memories yellowed, hardened,
like the doilies and antimacassars
she scattered to protect the furniture.

As she sank into solitude
the house acquired breath,
even speech, children's voices
and her husband calling her,
droning out the faint crash
of distant waves.

It now exudes a musty odor,
as chiaroscuro light seeps
through cloudy windows,
casts faint shadows on the floor
where threadbare carpets once lay,
worn thin by countless sandy feet.

The rooms are almost empty now
divested of mahogany furniture,
purged of photographs, portraits,
and possessions of her parents—
the gnarled walking stick,
the twisted art deco lamp,
the stuffed head of a buck,
preserved like sacred relics.

Still intact: the carved balustrade,
lintels over the doorways,
panes of Depression glass,
the veranda curled round the house
like a sleeping cat soaking up the sun.
She imagined it all would last forever.

Winter Chill

<u>Day</u>
The snarling wind attacks the trees,
upends those with shallow roots,
exposes them like carcasses
of eviscerated prey.

On a rampage, it breaks branches,
sends them tumbling down
to tear asunder electrical wires,
crash like cannon balls on roofs.

In the house the lights go off,
the temperature plummets,
but in the refrigerator it
creeps perversely upwards.

<u>Dusk</u>
As daylight dims, we rush
to gather candles, flashlights,
pile on layers of clothing
to protect us from the cold
insidiously infiltrating
our fragile fortress.

Reduced to elemental pursuits,
we light the small wood stove
in the basement, pull out an old
sofa bed and dive in to make heat.

<u>Night</u>
Bundled under quilts, we cling
and complain about the cold,
the inconvenient loss of power,
the inability to make coffee—

forget to pray for those
who huddle in doorways
on cardboard mattresses,
wrapped in torn, thin shrouds.

Recessional

Dressed in white like Druid priestesses
profaned with accents of class colors—
we form a long line stretching down the road
past the sun-drenched dogwoods and azaleas,
the paramecium pond studded with lilies,
the Gothic edifice casting its shadow.

At the head of the line, the class of 1938,
a handful of survivors, nonagenarians
riding in antique cars driven by young men.
Shakily they wave their hands, smile
as they pass the cheering throng.
Behind them, the march of the infirm
who cling to walkers, steer scooters,
roll wheel chairs, are pushed by others.

Each reunion we move up a notch,
and watch with wary interest 1958,
the class ahead, five years older,
note advanced signs of aging,
ominous harbingers of our own,
register the decreased number,
wonder how many chose not to come,
how many could not, calculate

who in five years might be missing.
Inverting the natural order of time,
the parade progresses from old to young
and ends with the class of 2008
screaming, jumping, wildly waving.
We applaud briefly, walk quickly away.

Actively Dying

My mother is "actively dying,"
as opposed to passively dying,
which is what the rest of us
are doing every day.
Actively dying—an oxymoron—
as if the energy of the body
shifts from preserving life
to extinguishing it.

Actively dying really means
the body has staged a coup
against the arrogant mind,
that delusional tyrant
twirling and whirling
his hollow scepter
like a child spinning a top,
who thinks he'll live forever
until the body revolts,
brings the old fool down.

Golf Links

Not having played for twenty years,
not since your last game,
I didn't die as you did, Daddy,
on the golf course, in the heat—
trying to keep up,
not wanting to break up
the foursome—
not wanting to complain
of the pain in the chest.

I didn't die as you did, Daddy,
but I felt close to you anyway,
my silent partner
out there on the fairway,
linked by the possibility
of an identical death,
the possibility of sinking
like a well-aimed putt
into the last hole.

Ashes

The marble urn is heavy,
its contents weightless.
I unscrew the lid, pour
my father into a bag,
turn my head away
to avoid inhaling the dust.

Next I open the wooden box
containing my mother,
neglected for too many years
for lack of instruction on her part,
lack of resolution on mine.
I empty the box into the same bag.

Together at last, I take them
to the bay they gazed at every day
from the windows of our house,
the bay they swam in every summer.

My cousin anchors at the spot
where we scattered his mother's ashes.
The day is warm and brilliant,
a celebratory sun ablaze on the water.

As I release them into the ocean,
watch the pale green bloom
form and drift away,
I yearn for solid ground.

Grave Side

In the cold drizzle of late November,
my husband and his sister lean
dutifully over their parents' grave,
knees planted on the wet lawn,
heads bowed, backs bent as if praying.

With a trowel my husband
digs up weeds and grass
growing around the marker,
encroaching on the names
with a thick, green shroud.

His sister brushes away
the soil with her hands,
and a frayed Kleenex,
scratches with manicured nails
the dirt stuck in the letters.

I wonder if they wonder
who else is the audience,
if their parents (even God!)
might be watching the scene,
as they perform this act
as a part they really feel.

Beatitude

A radiant spring day
in February.
My husband is in the garden
digging a grave.

The cat struggles to rise
from his dark hiding place
under the end table,
staggers to his water dish.

I have spent
much time, money,
on mindful meditation,
learning to live
in the moment.
I still don't get it.

Blessed are they
who do not know.

Diana **Loercher Pazicky** is a former English professor at Temple University and the author of a book, *Cultural Orphans in America*, based on her dissertation. Prior to receiving her doctorate, she was a full-time Staff Correspondent for ten years the *Christian Science Monitor* in Boston and New York. Having recently retired, she has been reveling in the freedom and opportunity to write poetry and plays. She lives in Bucks County, Pennsylvania with her husband, dog, and cat and is indebted to Chris Bursk and his poetry workshop at Bucks County Community College for their support and inspiration. She attempts in her poetry to incorporate a twist, an element of the unexpected, that provokes in the reader curiosity and a shift in perception. Her poems have been published in journals throughout the Pennsylvania/New Jersey area.

www.ingramcontent.com/pod-product-compliance
Lightning Source LLC
LaVergne TN
LVHW051611080426
835510LV00020B/3234